MW00941369

MUSINGS FROM COWBOY COUNTRY

GEORGE RHOADES

outskirtspress

DENVER, COLORADO

Outskirts Press, Inc.
http://www.outskirtspress.com

Paperback ISBN: 978-1-9772-0929-0

Library of Congress Control Number: 2019902174

Outskirts Press and the "OP" logo are trademarks belonging to Outskirts Press, Inc.

PRINTED IN THE UNITED STATES OF AMERICA

Contents

Beaver Creek

We needed rain, prayed for rain,
Wanted rain for the cotton and wheat,
But when it came, it came in buckets,
Fallin' and fallin' down in sheets.

Torrents and torrents far upstream
In the foothills of the Wichitas,
And the muddy red-dirt water
Came floodin' creeks and draws.

My Granny got out in a wagon,
The horses swimmin' part of the way;
Her little shanty remained in place;
Water got inside, three feet that day.

Her cows reached higher ground,
Turkeys and chickens in the trees,
Fences and posts washed away;
We waded out, water past our knees.

The barn, flimsy as it could be,
Leaned and crumpled on one side;
The chicken house was swept away
On the swiftly movin' reddish tide.

Beaver Creek flowed from its banks,
Spread across the valley floor
On its way south to the river,
Leavin' troubles by the score.

"Replant the wheat, save some cotton,
When the water finally goes down;
We've got a lot of work to do;
There ain't no use standin' around.

"Repair the barn and chicken coop,
Get the fences back in place,
Clean up the mud and fix the road,
And put a smile on your face."

That's what my grandmother said,
Tough and stoic and standin' tall,
That's what she did all her life,
That's how she got through it all.

Belly Up to the Bar

Belly up to the bar, boys,
Belly up to the bar.

Here we serve two drinks –
One is understanding,
The other is ignorance.

Ignorance is sweet,
And easy to go down;
Understanding is harder
To swallow –

Which will it be?

Beware, Beware

Grass is high,
Ponds are full,
Weather's fair –

Beef prices up,
Wheat's growin',
Birds singin' everywhere –

Livestock's fat,
Fences fixed,
Cool, refreshin' air –

Garden's green,
Money in the bank,
Not a care –

Hay all baled,
Calves branded,
No problems anywhere –

If it's too good
To be true,
Then beware, beware!

Brazos Bill,
The Stampede Man

Brazos Bill was the best, they said,
At takin' herds up the Chisholm Trail;
He did it for years and years,
And got 'em through without fail.

He knew the best waterin' places,
And where to bed 'em down,
And where to let 'em graze along
On the way to Abilene town.

Bill was master at crossin' streams
When they was flooded wide;
He knew all the longhorn tricks,
And he could rope and he could ride.

But he was the best there ever was
When cattle stampeded pell mell,
When they was "one jump and runnin'
And another jump to hell."

Bill was quick in the saddle,
He knew just what to do,
The best way to get 'em stopped,
And his big gelding, Streak, did too.

"You wanna know about stampedes?
I been in a few," Bill would say.
"A barkin' dog or a rattlin' pan,
Might send 'em on their way.

"Strikin' a match or a coyote's howl,
Any blessed thing under the sun,
Lightnin' or thunder or even a bird,
Might spook 'em, make 'em run.

"Once the moon came poppin' out
From behind a big cloud bank,
And the herd jumped and was fleein'
Afore we got around their flank.

"Even a jackrabbit jumpin' up
Could send 'em chargin' on,
Or a cowboy might sneeze,
And they'd be to hell and gone.

"What you gotta do," Bill would say,
"Hang on, hang on, hold on tight;
Trust your horse, trust your horse,
Even if it's the dead of night.

"You gotta get to the front,
Longhorns like to run to the right,
So you gotta ride to the left,
Get 'em millin', crowded tight."

It was close to Lookout Point
Where they had bedded 'em down,
Quiet and still and peaceful,
Night herders slowly ridin' around.

A cowboy's hat went blowin' off,
And the herd was runnin' like crazy,
Flattened the chuck wagon on the way
With cowhands flyin' 'cross the prairie.

They finally got 'em quieted down,
Churnin', turnin' in a calmin' mill;
They saw Streak off to one side,
Empty saddle, no sign of Bill.

He had fallen right in the middle
Where the longhorns stomped around;
They picked up his spurs and buckle,
Six-gun, but not much else was found.

That was how the saga ended:
Brazos Bill, best stampede man
Who ever traveled the long trail,
Was buried in a coffee can.

Close to the Flame

Shorty and Billy Bob,
Drinkin' at the Alamo Bar,
Were cussin' and discussin'
Subjects far and wide, near and far.

"What do you think,
Near as you can tell,"
Shorty asks, deep in thought,
"Is there really a heaven or a hell?"

"I don't rightly know,"
Billy Bob sez, sippin' his beer,
"But I kinda hope there's a hell,
'Cause it seems perfectly clear

"There's some what truly need
Punishin' for the deeds they do –
More'n what the law deals out –
They deserve the fiery pit, too.

"Them what kill little children,
And innocent people left and right,
Bomb and maim, massacre and slaughter,
Committin' evil day and night."

Shorty nods in agreement,
"But sometimes it seems to me,
There's so many of 'em down there,
It must be crowded as can be.

"And more arrivin' every day,
It's a real cryin' shame,
They might actually freeze
'Cause they can't get close to the flame."

Cottonwood Memories

Cottonwoods whisper,
Murmur on the breeze
Along the creek
Flowin' past the trees.

And they remember
From long, long ago:
Grass was high
And herds of buffalo.

Kiowas and Comanches
Rested in their shade,
Ridin' back from Mexico
After another raid.

Chisholm Trail cowhands,
Weary in the saddle,
Splashed in leafy shadow,
Watered longhorn cattle.

Pushin' the CR herd
On the way to Abilene;
The trees invitin',
Restful and serene.

The Texas cowboys,
Sunburned and tough,
Sought cool relief;
The trail hard and rough.

Cavalry troops camped
On the hills nearby,
Chasin' renegades,
Flags flyin' high.

Cottonwoods watched
The battle unfold;
Arrows and bullets,
Story largely untold.

Wagons headed west
Traveled along the stream,
Gathered wood and water,
On toward their dream.

Rustlers crossed here,
Runnin' from lawmen
Hot on their trail,
Ridin' hard, closin' in.

The stately cottonwoods
Were standin' there
When ranchers, farmers
Settled everywhere.

Big golden leaves
Fallin' to the ground;
White cottony fluff
Driftin', comin' down.

They saw the fences,
Pioneers and wire,
The plows and towns
Spread like fire.

Survivin' heat and cold,
Drought and wind,
Lightnin' and flood,
Storms without end.

In the far reaches
Of the ranch land,
Sturdy tall sentinels,
Majestic and grand.

Cottonwoods remember
Down through the years,
The struggles and triumphs,
The hopes and fears.

They murmur still,
Tellin' tales once more;
Listen, you can hear,
The old whispered lore.

Cowboy Ain't
A Dirty Word

I hear the word "cowboy"
Used more and more
As a put-down, an insult,
Something to deplore.

It's a trend I don't cotton to,
And it needs to halt,
"Cowboy" ain't a dirty word
Used to find fault.

The other day I read
Ecologists accusin' their foes
Of usin' "cowboy thinkin'"
Causin' environmental woes.

An oil firm was said,
In getting' drillin' rights,
To use "cowboy tactics"
To secure the sites.

He's "too cowboy"
One candidate claimed
About his opponent
Who should "be ashamed."

Story in a foreign press
Said the U.S. was guilty
Of "acting like a cowboy"
With too much hostility.

"Cowboy" used like this
Means somebody who's reckless,
Wild, brash, thoughtless,
Hotheaded and careless.

Somebody who'd take risks,
In a foolhardy way,
Court danger, be a daredevil,
Bringin' "hell to pay."

Now "cowboy" ain't a term
Of ridicule or disrespect;
For most, it's meaning is clear,
Carries special effect.

Cowboys herdin' longhorns
Created a reputation,
And became an icon,
And symbol for this nation.

Simple, direct and tough,
And not backin' down,
Doin' the best you can,
And standin' your ground.

Cowboys ain't reckless when
Takin' care of the herd,
When the chips are on the line,
Or when givin' their word.

Cowboys always got the herd
Through to Abilene,
Despite storms, stampedes
And everything in between.

"Cowboy" means to cinch up,
Stand tall, stay strong and free,
Git 'er done; that's what
"Cowboy" means to me.

Cowboy Christmas Day

Breakin' ice and haulin' hay
On a cowboy Christmas day,
Cactus, cedar and mesquite
Coated in ice and sleet.

Cattle all huddle together
Out of the frigid weather
Along the timber creek;
Skies gray and bleak.

A coyote wanders warily,
Prowlin' the woods cautiously
In the early-mornin' glow
Of freshly fallen snow.

North wind comes howlin,'
A sharp, whistlin' violin,
Screamin' like a banshee
Across the open prairie.

Stars the night before
Bright diamonds galore;
Trees standin' bare
In the cold wintry air.

Workin' way out here
Miles from anywhere,
Cold and bitter and raw
Down every hill and draw.

A lonely crow calls,
And the sound softly falls
Over the frosty range,
Eerie, hauntin' and strange.

"Thank God we get to see
This outdoor majesty,"
All the cowhands say
On a cowboy Christmas day.

Cowboy Malady

The doctors said, "You need therapy,
Out in the sun, away from stress."
So I took a job as a cowboy
To ease my mind, find saneness.

I was the greenest of greenhorns,
Didn't know much about a cow,
But they set me to chasin' strays,
Holdin' to the saddlehorn somehow.

My pony knew more than I did,
Quick and steady at runnin' 'em in;
I couldn't dodge the mesquite limbs,
Fell in prickly pear, scratched shin and skin.

Brandin', turnin' bull calves into steers,
Dirt and heat and holdin' 'em down;
They gave me the dirtest jobs of all,
Kicked and butted, knocked to the ground.

Sleepin' under the stars, out in the wind,
Sunburnt, aches and pains and bone tired;
But I kept hangin' on and hangin' on,
Doin' my best to keep from bein' fired.

So I was ridin' drag out on the trail,
When we finally got 'em pointed north,
Dust and dust and more dust filled the air,
Across the Brazos to the pens in Fort Worth.

Coffee black and strong, tin cup and plate,
Beans, beef and bacon three times a day,
Night-herdin' when stars are shinin' bright,
Up at dawn and we're on our way.

Storms came sweepin' down the prairie,
Rain and flood, thunder, lightnin' and hail,
Then on one dark and threatenin' night,
They ran, stampeded, scattered up the trail.

We rode and rode, finally got 'em to millin',
Tallied up the losses, headed north again,
Then I thought I'd never make it,
Trail-herdin' and cowboyin' had me all in.

Livin' in a ramshackle line shack,
Roundin' 'em up, fixin' fence, haulin' hay,
Pullin' calves, breakin' ice in the winter,
Givin' it all I had and then some everyday.

I learned to rope and to ride,
To stay in the saddle and get back on,
And see the beauty in the rollin' hills,
The endless sky and the fiery dawn.

When I dragged myself back to the doctors,
After months of livin' as a drover,
They said my original ailment was gone,
But I had a new one I might never get over.

The doctors said best they could tell
What I had was a strange new malady:
It had taken control of my very bein' –
And now a cowpoke was all I'd ever be.

Cowboys Ain't Preachers

Cowboys ain't preachers,
They might say a prayer though
When they're straddlin' a bull
In the chute, ready to go.

They might tell a funny joke
That's a bit off-color and blue,
And make church ladies blush,
But it gets a laugh or two.

They've been known to take a drink
In a grubby saloon or bar,
And even have a few too many,
That's just the way things are.

They often skip goin' to church
More'n just once in a while,
They're busy out workin' cattle,
Not doin' anything evil or vile.

They often listen to cowboy songs –
"Cowboy's Prayer" or "Master's Call," –
Sung by Johnny Cash or Marty Robbins,
And many songs not religious at all.

Cowboy theology is fairly simple:
Follow the Good Book if you can,
But sometimes that can't be done,
Surely the Good Lord will understand.

Cowboys live and do their work
Way out where they can see
All around them all the time
The Lord's handiwork abundantly.

The prairie sweeps to the horizon,
The sky arches high overhead,
Sunset and sunrise colors splash
Yellow, orange and fiery red.

They hear the lonely coyote cry,
The wind whisperin', moanin' low,
See the grass wavin' in the breeze,
Watch the night's starry show.

They'd like to go to heaven,
But say they've already been there
When they're ridin' high and wide
On the prairie, breathin' prairie air.

Cowboys ain't preachers;
They really don't need to be
'Cause on the trail they've seen
The grandeur of God's Country.

Cowboys Are Comin'

The word would spread
All around the town,
The cow herds are comin';
Get ready, buckle down.

Line up the whiskey bottles,
Polish up the bar,
Tune up the fiddles,
Bring out the guitar.

The cowboys are comin';
They're bringin' in the cattle;
They're crossin' the Arkansas
After months in the saddle.

Dusty, scruffy and thirsty,
Headin' for a wing-ding blast,
The wild Texas cowhands
Reachin' Abilene at last.

Rip-roarin' and raisin' hell,
The U2 and the Circle R,
Comin' with the longhorns;
Put some sawdust on the floor.

Tell Miss Emily's girls
They need more powder and paint;
Tell the faro dealers, crap shooters,
No time to show restraint.

Alert the sheriff and the marshal
To tidy up the city jail,
The first herds are on the way,
Comin' up the Chisholm Trail.

All the way from down in Texas,
The herds are flowin' north,
Crossin' the Brazos and the Red,
Movin' past old Fort Worth.

The cowhands are ridin' in,
Wantin' hats, boots and stuff,
And when they get paid off,
They'll spend it fast enough.

Dairy Queen Cowboy

He drives a Ford Ranger,
Ropes, wires, waterbag, canteen,
Old metal posts in the bed
When he parks at Dairy Queen.

He orders up a root beer,
Sits and drinks it solemnly;
He's decked out head to toe,
Sharp and cowboy as can be.

Nocona boots brown and white
Swirls stitched on the side,
Roper's heel and square toed
Made from tough cowhide.

Cowboy straw curled up
Broad brim and high crown,
Beaded black and red hatband,
Ivory-colored, all pulled down.

Wrangler boot-cut jeans,
Bought from J.C. Penney,
Sharp crease, firm fittin',
For wearin' free and easy.

Engraved wide leather belt,
Buckle a silvery lone star,
Flashy, bright and shinin',
Lookin' big as a boxcar.

Light blue Western shirt,
Embroidered rose whirl,
Long sleeves, tail tucked in,
Ruby red snaps of pearl.

He saddles a table in the back,
Talks about Cheyenne and Denver,
Calgary and Amarillo, too,
But he ain't been there ever.

Boots are clean like new,
Jeans without a cowlot stain,
Hat unsoiled by grime and sweat,
Shirt crisp, showin' no strain.

The girls at the Dairy Queen,
Say he's a really cute cowboy
In his bright, colorful garb
Like old photos of Gene and Roy.

The only thing he rounds up
Is in the parkin' lot at Walmart,
Where he carefully rides herd
On any stray shoppin' cart.

And at his second job,
He sells cigarettes and gasoline,
Then follows the windin' trail
Across town to Dairy Queen.

Day of the Cowboy

Day of the Cowboy
In the hot July
At the Chisholm museum
Honorin' times gone by.

Pony rides for the kids,
Longhorns in a pen,
Chuck wagon set up
Just like back then.

Ropers and storytellers,
Displays on the grounds,
Cowboy band strummin'
Western songs and sounds.

Cowboy Day visitors
Listenin' to the tales
Of herds movin' north
Up the old cattle trails.

Cowboy hats and boots,
Belt buckles, blue jeans,
Colorful shirts, bandanas,
Hot dogs and pinto beans.

Tents and tables spread
In the cool, cool shade,
Featurin' authentic gear
Of the cowboy trade.

Fancy saddles, spurs,
Sixguns in a case,
Things from the past
Once were commonplace.

A rawhide lariat,
A Bowie knife or two,
An old Mexican bridle,
Fiddles and guitar, too.

Barb wire strands,
Brands on a board,
Cattle drive paintin'
That won an award.

Different kinds of chaps –
Stovepipes and batwings,
Leather whips, harness bells,
Stirrups and saddle strings.

Festival and ceremony,
Cheerful celebration
To honor the legendary
Icon of this nation.

Museum sits now
Along the very track
Chisholm Trail drovers
Traveled on horseback.

They trailed the herds
From the Lone Star state.
Sweatin', dusty, weary,
To the loadin' gate.

The oldtime cowhands
Would be shocked to see
That what they did then
Lives now in history.

Folks payin' homage,
Keepin' memory alive
Of the heroic days
Of the old cattle drive.

So once a year
A day is set aside –
The Day of the Cowboy
Observed far and wide.

But to tell the truth,
It takes more'n a day
To pay proper tribute
To cowboys of yesterday.

Days of the Camel

Ain't it funny
How things turn out?
How things
Come about?

There coulda
Been long-necked,
Long-legged
Beasts unchecked,

Roamin' around
All over the West,
Hard to catch,
Strange at best.

Just like herds
Of swift mustangs,
Loose and free,
Runnin' in gangs.

One or two humped,
Fast as a horse,
Days without water,
Camels, of course.

The Army brung 'em
Many years ago
To West Texas
Goin' to-and-fro.

Spittin' and bitin',
The dromedaries
Carried heavy loads
Across the prairies.

Hard to handle,
Scary to see,
The big experiment
Failed eventually.

Thus ended
The camel corps;
The odd creatures
Were no more.

There coulda been
Camels at the rail,
Or drivin' longhorns
Up the Chisholm Trail.

If they'd prevailed,
Old cowhands
Might've saddled up
Ships of the sands.

Desperation and Anxiety

Desperation and anxiety
Came calling today,
I didn't know
What to say.

Thank the Lord, though,
For the attractions,
Amusements to put them off –
The pretty distractions.

I-phones and I-pads,
Videos and giant screens,
Boob tube, surfing the net,
Bemusing by any means.

They left me alone
After a while
To play my games
And smile my smile.

Dinosaur Tracks

"Those are dinosaur tracks
In the rock by the river's edge,
Millions of years old, ain't it somethin'?
They walked on a muddy ledge,"

Shorty said to Billy Bob
In the scrub oak and mesquite,
As they chased strays in the brush
Through the Texas summer heat.

"The tracks hardened, turned to stone,
And there they are for us to see.
More'n sixty million years ago,
Dinosaurs ruled completely.

"Some were big as barns,
There were little ones, too.
They ran around in herds,
Some had wings and flew."

"What happened to 'em?" Billy Bob said.
"Why," Shorty replied, "they all died
When a big fireball came down
Hit the earth and they all fried."

"And," Shorty told Billy Bob,
"All of 'em wiped out, all the herds.
Nothin' left but a few little ones,
And they turned into birds."

"Birds? They turned into birds?"
Billy Bob asked with a grin,
"And they're flyin' around now?
Shorty, have you been drinkin' again?"

Do Cowboys Matter Still

Do cowboys matter still
In a time of gloom and doom,
A time of anxiety and strife?

Cowboys tall in the saddle,
Standin' alone against the odds,
Facin' danger, not backin' down,
Overcomin' storms, floods, stampedes,
Ragin' rivers, quicksand and wind,
Lightnin', hail, rattlesnakes, too –
Nature's wild fury itself –
To get the herd through.

Prevailin' against outlaws,
Greedy cattle barons, rustlers,
Raiders, baddies of every stripe –

But the cowboy wasn't perfect,
He wasn't a saint,
He got drunk, raised hell in cowtowns,
Shot it out with other cowboys,
Went to houses of ill repute,
Gambled in saloons and some
Become desperadoes on the run,
Reckless, ridin' the outlaw trail.

Despite all the flaws, the cowboy –
The image, legend, myth and mystique –
Became the great American folk hero.

Not the lumberjack or the farmer,
The mountaineer, miner, fisherman,
Shopkeeper or the steelworker –
It was the cowboy who grabbed
The imagination of the nation;
Cowboys on horseback, big hats,
Janglin' spurs, chaps, boots, six-shooters,
Rode into the country's heart and soul.

Americans yearned to be resilient,
Forthright, self-reliant, independent,
Adventurous – like the cowboy.

Courageous horsemen, livin' a life
Of danger, drivin' wild longhorns,
Across the hot, hostile plains,
Strong, practical, resourceful,
Believin' in freedom and liberty,
Rugged individuals, high-spirited,
Tamin' the frontier wilderness,
Makin' do despite hardships.

The cowboy spirit was there
With energy and determination
To get through World Wars,
The Great Depression, Dust Bowl,
Civil strife, Korea and Vietnam,
The Cold War, wars and more wars,
Ups and downs and divisive discord
And clashes of every kind.

But the question remains:
Do cowboys matter still
Like they did once upon a time?

Don't Cry, Juanita

Hold my hand, Juanita,
When we cross the ragin' water,
Hold my hand, Rosalita,
Comin' down the mountains
Of Honduras and Guatemala,
And on the hot journey
Through the deserts of Mexico
To Potosi and Chihuahua.

We're doin' hard travelin'
From Puerto Barrios
Past the dark jungles
And long, long roads;
Don't cry, Juanita;
Hold my hand,
Headed for the Promise Land.

Don't cry, Juanita,
Don't cry for the Sierra Madre
And the lost Rio Dulce.
Hold my hand, don't cry, Rosalita,
We'll find a new home
Where mother freedom
Stands like a beacon,
Lifts her lamp beside the golden door.

Dream Ride

The old cowboy sat in the chair,
A blanket across his lap,
On the patio of the rest home,
Wakin' from his nap.

I did 'em all, he said,
Ridin' and ropin' at the rodeo
All up and down the line,
Calgary to Cheyenne to El Paso.

Now I'm crippled up and stuck
With caretakers and fadin' memory,
Thinkin' back on the past,
Gone forever now for me.

But when I sleep I dream
That I'm buckin' once again,
A small town, flags aflyin',
Tryin' my best to win.

Corrals, horses, pickup trucks,
Spurs, buckles, chaps and ropes,
Arenas, bulls, barrel racers,
Livin' on dreams and hopes.

Travelin' from town to town,
Wantin' to make the short go,
To get the cash and the glory;
Hard life, not much to show.

Comin' outta the chute,
One arm up, under stormy sky,
Hat pulled low, holdin' tight,
Pickup man waitin' nearby.

I've drawn a good one,
Bronc with lots of fire,
High-kickin' and high-jumpin',
I'm ridin' 'im higher and higher.

Settlin' into the rhythm,
Day money's gonna be mine,
Spurrin' on a high roller,
Pains forgotten, feelin' fine.

The roar from the crowd,
Ride 'em cowboy, comes the cry,
The cheers urge me on
As I grab for the sky.

Then I hear the buzzer,
Eight-second ride and top score;
My dream comes to an end
'Til I dream it all once more.

Drovers in Heaven

Billy Bob and Shorty hunkered
Around the campfire at night,
Discussin' and philosophizin'
About the world and its plight –

"Do you think up there in heaven
They got cattle drives and cowhands,"
Billy Bob asks, solemn and somber,
"Crossin' the heavenly promise lands?"

"Why, of course, they surely do,"
Shorty says, speakin' with certainty.
"We know the Devil has a herd,
So does the Good Lord most assuredly.

"I dreamt about goin' there once,"
Shorty says, gazing at the sky.
"And it was a beautiful place,
A lot like Texas, to my eye.

"Only the longhorns up there
Ain't fire-eyed and runnin' wild,
They're tame as little kittens,
And movin' along meek and mild.

"And there ain't no stampedes,
And the rivers are all ankle deep,
And quicksand is hard and firm,
And from rustlers not a peep.

"All the hosses are fast as lightnin'
And come right up when you call,
They know how to turn a steer,
Cut 'em out, and they never fall.

"The saddles are made of silver,
And the bridles are all gold,
And days and nights on horseback
Never get tiresome or old.

"And there ain't no scorchin' heat,
Icy winds or storms sweepin' through
With hail and floods and blindin' rains
Makin' life miserable for you.

"And when they deliver the herd
To the pens at the end of the trail,
They can celebrate a little bit,
'Cause there ain't no sheriff or jail.

"The saloons are cheerful friendly,
And the drinks are all free,
And the drovers can go back home
With all their pay, happy as can be.

"I been thinkin' that that dream
Was more'n just a dream –
It was more like a message
From above, it would seem.

"The Good Lord was sayin'
We need to change our ways –
Stop getting' drunk and raisin' hell,
Repent for the rest of our days.

"Or we'll be ridin' down below
Chasin' after that Devil's herd,
Wishin' we'd paid more attention
To the Good Book and the Good Word."

Eau de Billy Goat

Odors can trigger memories,
Bring back intense recollections
Of things from the past,
Rememberances and reflections.

When I smell somethin' bakin',
I clearly and sharply recall
My Granny's warm kitchen –
Biscuits, cookies, cakes and all.

Freshly plowed up red dirt
Reminds me of long-gone days
Ridin' the old John Deere,
Blazin' sun and mornin' haze.

But it works in reverse, too,
A memory can trigger a smell
That comes back pungently,
Sharp like a ringin' bell.

Movin' cattle place to place,
I had to keep 'em straight
And not turn in at Reed's farm,
A chore I learned to hate.

The Reeds had a billy goat;
He'd come out to greet me,
When I was onfoot keepin'
'Em movin' along swiftly.

I can see him even now;
I had to shove him away
When he tried to headbutt me,
Maybe just his idea of play.

He'd stare at me with eyes
Strange enough to horrify;
I'd grab his horns and push
'Til the cows got safely by.

But it's billy's odor
That comes back most vile
When I remember those days
Every once in a while.

The putrid repulsive smell
Floated along in the air
When billy walked on out
To where I was standin' there.

A forgotten stench triggered
By thoughts, I'd like to note,
Of past times, movin' cows –
And eau de billy goat.

Fearless Bull Rider

The old bull rider leaned his cane
Against the bar, sippin' his beer,
Straddlin' a barstool, talkin'
To the cowboys gathered there.

He'd been a top money-winner
At ridin' them bulls long ago,
Ranked Number One for years,
The champ, don't you know?

"They said I was 'fearless,'
That I absolutely had no fear,
That bulls didn't scare me,
I could ride 'em, that was clear.

"When I climbed into the chute,
I looked confident and strong,
Settlin' down on his back,
Best bull rider to come along.

"The papers said I was the greatest,
The way I tipped my hat,
The way I hung for the ride,
The fame, the glory, and all that.

"I rode 'em all across the country,
From Houston up to Calgary,
From back east to way out west,
From Chicago down to Miami.

"Broke both my legs in Vegas,
Arm and ribs in old Cheyenne,
Broken bones too many to count,
I was a ridin' fool back then.

"I won lots of big ones, too,
Buckles, trophies and tons of dough;
I loved it when the crowd cheered,
When I was a star of the rodeo.

"But I got a confession to make –
I weren't 'fearless' like they said,
Fear had a tight hold on me,
But I went on, I went ahead.

"Gettin' onto an angry ton
Of buckin', kickin', beast,
That's tryin' to gore ya, kill ya,
Ain't funny, to say the least.

"Right up until I got too old,
I never knew if I could do it,
If I could overcome the fear,
And not choke, give up and quit.

"When you've pulled the rope tight,
At that point there's no doubt,
This is it, keep a grip, hold on,
There's no way to back out.

"Bein' scared plumb to death,
And goin' ahead anyway,
Tryin' to show I weren't afraid –
That's how I lived day to day."

Goodbye Memory

Old Amos sat in a wheelchair
At the nursin' home,
Talkin' about the bygone days
When he used to roam
From ranch to ranch, bustin' broncs,
Ridin' in the rodeo
Up and down the river valley,
Top hand years ago.

He said he remembered me,
But I wasn't sure –
He said the doctors told him,
There wasn't any cure;
It was dementia or senility
Or probably alzheimers
That was workin' on him hard –
What they called "old-timers."

"I can't remember things," he said.
"It's all goin' away –
Fadin' out, all the recollections,
Memories from yesterday.
The more I try to bring 'em back,
The more I find that I'm
Just pullin' up an empty bucket
About an olden time.

"Saddlin' old Pard and movin'
Cows across Beaver Creek
To the pastures on the other side
As grass starts to peak –
That's something I'd really like
To be able to recall –
The way the calves frolicked
When the bluestem was tall.

"Even the icy winter winds,
The scorchin' summer heat,
Blowin' dust and tumbleweeds,
The green of winter wheat,
Are memories I hate to lose –
Things I'm no longer knowin',
In this awful fog of forgettin',
My mind's slowly goin'.

"The hawks circlin' high above,
The scissortails in the air,
Cottonwoods and mesquite in bloom,
The prairie spread everywhere.
The silent nights, the red-dirt hills,
Moonlight's golden glow,
The stars bright as diamonds,
The cold before the snow.

"The way it felt hangin' on
For an eight-second ride,
To win the gold and the glory,
To feel the cowboy pride.
To live and work all my life
With horses and cattle,
Under the great sweepin' sky –
Livin' in the saddle.

"The storm clouds sweepin' in –
Thunder and lightnin', too,
I really want to keep rememberin'
If that's possible to do.
I hope the last to fade away –
The last about this land –
Was what I saw and did
When I was a cowhand."

GPS Devices on Cows?

They're puttin' GPS devices
In the eartags of cows –
To track where they go –
Visits to feed and waterin' holes,
Weight, reactions to weather, etc.,
Givin' ranchers lots of info.

How long before the devices
Are put on me and you?
To track where we go –
Visits to feed and waterin' holes,
Weight, reactions to weather, etc.,
Givin' the world lots of info.

Grandpa

I was eight, Grandpa was ninety-eight
That summer on the farm;
My job to see he didn't wander off,
Get lost or come to any harm.

He wore a heavy shirt, buttoned to the top,
Wrinkled khaki pants, faded cowboy hat,
Scruffy boots, smoked a smelly pipe;
I still remember him like that.

They said he'd been a cowboy
In the days of long ago,
But that was hard for me to grasp,
Hard for me to know.

Back then my idea of cowboys
Was shaped by Roy and Gene,
Singin' and playin' guitars,
Ridin' across the silver screen.

The Durango Kid all in black,
Fancy saddles, horses marvelous to see,
Sparkly rhinestone shirts, jinglin' spurs,
That's what cowboys meant to me.

Stalwart heroes of the plains,
Who beat up bad guys in saloons,
Won the hearts of pretty girls
Under starry skies and silvery moons.

So I didn't listen when he tried
To tell about the bygone years,
About big roundups in Texas,
Drivin' north longhorn steers.

I didn't pay any attention
To his mumbled stories of the trail,
Crossin' rivers, quicksand, stampedes,
Blindin' rains, howlin' winds and hail.

He told of loadin' pens in Abilene,
But I didn't listen to what he said,
He told of prairie fires, heat and dust,
The flooded Cimarron and the ragin' Red.

He passed away that fall,
One of the last of an oldtime breed;
Now I regret to his final words
I didn't listen, I didn't heed.

He Came Back

He kept goin' back
And goin' back
To Afganistan
And Iraq,
Wantin' to serve
Like his daddy did,
Like his uncles
And granddad did.

For adventure
And country,
Young and strong,
Eager as could be;
The uniform
He proudly wore
And did his
Patriotic chore.

They played taps,
Held a parade;
He rests now
In graveyard shade
After he
Came back
From Afganistan
And Iraq.

Hello, Death

Well, hello, Death,
What do you have to say
For yourself,
After all the fear and anxiety
You have caused?

You're the reason
For all the weird,
Fantastic, strange
Philosophies that bedevil
The human race.

You have given rise
To countless odd speculations
Designed to ease the dread and terror –
And to answer the question:
What comes after you?

What if by some twist
Of the mind,
We didn't know about you?
Wouldn't we be better off?
And live happier lives?

I Don't Like Lonely

I don't like ridin' far
In a car,
Sittin' in a traffic jam,
That's just who I am.

I don't like music loud,
A noisy crowd,
Long ticket lines,
Or even porcupines.

And I don't like lonely,
That's not for me,
When you're away,
It's a gloomy day.

Nothin' ain't right,
Not by a damn sight,
When lonely's here,
And you're not near.

I Never Liked the Rodeo

"I never liked the rodeo,"
The old cowboy said to me,
"But I've done it all my life,
It's where I always wanted to be.

"I've been in rodeos, big and small,
From Cheyenne to Denver to Amarillo,
Winnin' some and losin' some,
But I never liked it, don't you know?

"I never liked climbin' on the back
Of an angry bull that's tryin'
To stomp me, gore me, kick me,
Doin' his best to leave me dyin'.

"I don't like the buckin' broncs,
Twistin', jumpin', tougher'n hell,
And all the sounds and smells,
I never really liked them as well.

"Ropin' and ridin' never did appeal
To me much over the years,
Even though I made a livin'
Despite all the pain and fears.

"I never liked the sleepless nights
Drivin' from town to town,
Always scramblin', on the go,
And never ever settlin' down.

"The steer wrestlin' and calf ropin'
Never was what I wanted to do,
And the bruises and broken bones
Weren't much fun, I tell you.

"So, you ask, why did I do it?
What kept me ridin' again and again?
Comin' outta the chute once more,
Even when I had no chance to win?

"It was the people who brought me back;
I liked the bronc busters and bulldoggers,
The bullriders, ropers and barrel racers,
And the clowns and the steer-wrestlers.

"I liked their crazy dare-devil spirit,
Their rough-and-ready style and show,
I liked being around those folks,
That's what kept me followin' the rodeo."

If Billy Could
See It Now

Billy the Kid keeps ridin'
across the American landscape –
there are museums from
deep in the heart of Texas
to Lincoln and Fort Sumner in New Mexico.

Visitor centers and gift shops,
scenic byways and highways,
a casino and a car show,
auto repair and landscaping firms
and businesses of every kind
keepin' his name alive.

Books roll off the presses –
Gore Vidal, Larry McMurtry
and even Pat Garrett have penned
works about "The Kid,"
one of the most written-about
characters in American history.

Movies by the score
have played on the nation's screens –
Paul Newman, Robert Taylor,
Val Kilmer, Kris Kristofferson
have all portrayed Billy.

He was a major character
in flicks by Roy and Gene;
Howard Hughes made
"The Outlaw," featurin' Jane Russell,
Audie Murphy, who knew about guns,
played Billy as well.

Songs about Billy fill the airways –
Marty Robbins, Billy Joel, Dylan,
Woody Guthrie and Charlie Daniels, too,
have sung about the young gunfighter.

A tintype of Billy holdin'
his Colt and Winchester
sold for $2 million,
and a photo of him playing croquet
is worth millions more, they say.

Vicious killer or romantic figure of the West?
the truth is hard to find;
Aaron Copland composed a ballet
about "Billy the Kid,"
O. Henry based his hero,
"The Cisco Kid" on Billy.

"The Kid" has been a fixture
on TV shows – played by
Robert Vaughan and Robert Blake –
on Gunsmoke, Death Valley Days
and many, many more.

Billy's grave is in Fort Sumner,
tombstone stolen often;
rumors fly that he
wasn't really killed, but lived on
for years in Texas or Nevada or Kansas,
facts murky, hard to prove.

Posters and post cards of Billy
with his guns sell like hot cakes,
coffee cups, coasters, key chains,
trinkets of every description feature
Billy's image and fill gift shops

Billy spoke fluent Spanish,
liked to sing and dance,
quick on the draw
and deadly accurate,
blue-eyed and a charmer, the story goes,
the girls loved him –

And the saga is told and retold,
and the legend refuses to die.

If Fate Had Been Kinder

If we coulda been
What we wanted to be,
We woulda been cowboys
Ridin' the sagebrush sea.

If fate had been kinder
To you and me,
We woulda been out there
On the lone prairie.

It woulda been roundups,
Horses and cattle,
Spurs and hats, takin' 'em north,
Life in the saddle.

If fate had been kinder
At shapin' our road,
We woulda been cowboys,
Livin' the cowboy code.

If It Wasn't for Longhorns

If it wasn't for the longhorn,
There wouldn't be no cowboy myth,
No stories and legends and songs about
Cowhands to ride the river with.

What if the rugged longhorns
Had been mild Holsteins instead?
Would the roundups in South Texas
Have gone unnoticed, the yarns unsaid?

The longhorn was big and tough,
Aggressive, angry, sharp-horned and mean,
The kind of beast that made for
An awesome sight and dramatic scene.

If the cowboys had been herdin'
Docile milk cows up the Chisholm Trail,
What kind of story would have been told?
Would it have been a stirrin' tale?

The longhorn, raised on prickly pear,
Mesquite and thorns under a blazin' sun,
Lived with rattlesnakes, cactus, coyotes,
Always ready to fight or run.

It took cowboys just as tough
To drive 'em a thousand miles or more
Over rough terrain, flooded rivers,
Stampedes and hardships by the score.

They say Texas longhorn cattle,
When it came to makin' do,
Could leave other breeds in the dust
And they'd always make it through.

So the longhorn helped create
The great American cowboy hero,
When the free-ranging longhorn herds
Thundered out of Texas long, long ago.

If those cattle had been gentle
Jersey dairy cows makin' the drive,
The legendary epic saga of the West
Would never have come alive.

If You Make It to 80...

If you make it to 80,
And you can walk and talk,
Hear and see and are not an invalid,
Thank your lucky stars –

If you make it to 90,
And you can do those things,
And you can feel and comprehend,
Thank whatever gods there may be –

And if you make to 100,
Still seeing, hearing, walking, talking,
Thank luck, the stars, the gods,
And the very universe itself.

I'll Never Ride
The Rodeo Again

Though the flags are flyin' high
And crowds are cheerin', my friend,
There's one thing that I know:
I'll never ride the rodeo again.

She came up from Waco,
Texas prairies in her eyes,
She was quick and graceful fine
Ridin' under Texas skies.

Yellow hair, ready smile,
She stole my heart that day,
Runnin' the barrels, flashin' past,
Elegant beauty on display.

We followed the rodeo road,
Me and my gal from Waco,
Livin' out our joyous dreams,
Feelin' our love grow and grow.

I rode the buckin' broncs,
On Blaze, she ran the barrels;
We saw the bright lights,
Heard the ringin' of the bells.

From Arizona down to Houston,
From El Paso town to Calgary,
We traveled and roamed far and wide,
Our love carried us wild and free.

There's Cheyenne and San Antone,
And the Fort Worth Stock Show,
Tucson, Las Vegas, Pendleton,
Tulsa, Dodge City and Reno.

But I'll never ride the rodeo again;
In the Denver arena I lost her,
Blaze stumbled on the turn and fell;
Memory now a terrible, awful blur.

I live in this lonely place,
Out where the lonely wind
Sobs and moans in the cactus;
I'll never ride the rodeo again.

Justice and Politics

Justice is blind, they say,
And politics makes strange
Bedfellows –
And the two seldom meet.

Politics is an unruly game
Played everywhere,
Justice is measured
And hard to find
Anywhere.

Knock 'im back, Billy Joe

Windy and cold autumn night,
Out on the edge of town,
People crowded in the stands,
Along the sidelines up and down.

Hometown battling its arch rival,
Young athletes hitting, smashing,
Blocking, tackling, running, pushing,
Under the lights, stalwarts clashing.

Big farm kid comes off the field,
Bulked up in helmet, pads and all,
Little farm woman grabs his arm,
Pleads in her West Texas drawl:

"Billy Joe, you got to stop 'im,
Don't let him get in there,
Knock 'im back, knock 'im back;
Hit 'im low, hit 'im square."

"Okay, Ma, okay, Ma," he says.
He missed the block on bootleg right.
"I'll get 'im next time, Ma,
I'll knock 'im back, I'll hit him tight."

Cheerleaders prancing along the side,
Working hard, working the crowd;
High school band blasting away,
School fight song, booming loud.

Goal line stand, hold the line,
Don't fumble, attack, attack!
Fight, fight for the team;
Knock 'im back, knock 'im back.

Defense! Defense! comes the cry,
Last down, not another yard,
Shove and drive and collide,
Hit 'em low and hit 'em hard.

Return the punt, third and long,
Move the chain, field goal try,
For bragging rights, inside run,
'Git 'im, git 'im', it's do or die.

Out on the West Texas prairie,
A Friday night story,
Victory or defeat, win or lose,
Knock 'im back, run to glory.

Last of the Strays

We rounded up the strays,
The ones that got away
When we herded 'em to the pens
For the final sale day.

The spread was shuttin' down,
The old Circle R was through;
They sold off the horses,
And most of the cattle, too.

A hundred years or more
Strugglin' on the Texas plains,
Years of drought, low cow prices,
Too many losses, too few gains.

They sold it all that day,
And the lively auction drew
From all around the county;
The crowd was more'n a few.

Hay bales and wheat drills,
Farmall tractors and John Deeres,
Along with mowers and combines
Sold off by the auctioneers.

Headgates and portable chutes,
All the gear sold and gone;
The ranch owners beaten down,
Tired of hangin' on and hangin' on.

Big ranchers bought the cows,
Bankers took the land,
The old Circle R faded away;
It had made its last stand.

Cowboys finished up their chores,
Said farewell and headed out;
Range gettin' smaller and smaller,
Times are changin', no doubt.

The final things to go
On that melancholy day,
Was the last of the strays,
The ones that almost got away.

Little Red Wagon

In back of the barn,
under old boxes, a tattered tarp,
rusty, paint peeling, dented,
one wheel missing, handle broken,
the little red wagon,
the Radio Flyer,
from my childhood days.

Then it was more
than a little red wagon –
it was a stagecoach riding
with Gene Autry,
a covered wagon
crossing the plains headed west.

A racecar, a space ship
traveling with Flash Gordon,
a tank with General Patton
smashing through the hedgerows,
a landing barge hitting
the beach with U.S. Marines.

It carried sacks of grain
out to the chicken coops,
potatoes from the garden,
buckets, wires, tools around the farm,
pets and kids up and down hills,
and once a block of ice
wrapped in tow sacks
from the store a mile away
to my granny's ice box.

It was the Batmobile
zooming with Batman and Robin,
a train headed to California,
a souped-up roadster
chasing Bonnie and Clyde,
an airplane carrying Jack Armstrong,
a chuckwagon on the Chisholm Trail,
a ship out on the high seas
sailing with Captain Kidd.

It was without limits;
knowledge is power, they say,
knowledge is something,
but imagination is everything –
it was my little red wagon.

Lives in the City Now

He said he lives in the city now,
Locks and chains and bars,
Gated community, punched in code,
Crowds, noise and rivers of cars.

"There ain't no lightnin' bugs
On still summer nights
Flashin' in my backyard,
Just glow from city lights.

"And I can't see the stars
That used to sparkle so
When the dark covered us,
A dazzlin' glimmerin' show.

"And the breeze smells of diesel
And the wind of gasoline,
And the hum of the interstate
Hangs outside my window screen.

"My life's in the city now,
Tho' I dream of bygone days,
Lightnin' bugs and starry skies,
And long gone country ways."

Livin' in Tornado Alley

We watched with dread and hope
As dark clouds churnin'
Built up over the western ridge
Roilin' toward us turnin'.

We know about the weather,
Livin' here in tornado alley –
Twisters can shatter giant trees,
Turn sturdy houses into debris.

The contrast stunnin' to behold,
The sky so blue and clear,
Then swiftly ominously darker,
Tension fillin' the atmosphere.

We're always needin' rain
In this part of the world,
But the clouds rolled angrily,
Lightnin' flashed, blackness swirled.

Comin' outta the southwest,
Like an out-of-control train,
Sweepin' across the valley,
And over the flatland plain.

We got the horses in the barn,
Stood in the storm cellar door;
Anxiety growin', fear, apprehension,
Listenin' to the oncomin' roar.

Wind picked up, blew harder,
Buckets of rain came down,
Thunder crashed louder and louder,
Water soaked the parched ground.

Nature in all its awesome power;
There was a beauty to it –
Trees swayed, outbuildings shook
As the wailin' stormfront hit.

The threat loomed over us,
Rotatin', revolvin', surgin' strong,
Furious skies, dangerous, menacin',
Screamin' out a perilous song.

The sky curled, twisted above,
Purple and green and black as night,
Down below we cringed, cowered,
Tryin' to hide out of sight.

Out along the whirlin' edge,
A funnel dipped, then went away,
Hangin' there briefly, terrible –
We're spared for another day.

A broken fence, tree limbs down,
But no real damage done,
Ponds, streams and lakes replenished,
Waitin' now for the returnin' sun.

The storm thundered on its way,
Smashin' across the prairie;
We're left alone to clean up,
Livin' here in tornado alley.

Looking Out, Looking Back

Looking out my back window
At the sleet, ice and snow,
And looking back at the past
Of days long, long ago –

My faint image in the glass
Floats on the wintry mists,
Reflections and recollections
Of life's turns and twists –

What kind of life have I lived?
Have I really been in the game,
Or have I been on the fringes
Too afraid, too timid, too tame?

Should I have been bolder,
Going more my own way,
And not so much concerned
With what others do and say?

Have I made the journey
With little to regret?
Or have I caused damage
To those that I met?

It's hard for me to tell,
As the finish line nears,
What my final tally shows
After all these many years.

Macho Stuff
Ain't Workin'

In a dingy bar in old Fort Worth,
An old cowboy drawled his Texas drawl,
And said to me, mutterin' low,
"I'm tellin' you I've seen it all.
I'm the way I've been for years,
But this romper-stomper macho stuff
Don't seem to be workin' much anymore.
I'm still smokin', drinkin', dippin' snuff,

"But the chicks nowadays don't dig it
Like they did in my younger days;
They want these prissy city fellers,
Polished up with sophisticated ways.
I still drive my old pickup truck,
Spit and chew and ride the rodeo,
Huntin' and fishin' like I used to do.
Gettin' drunk and loud, don't you know?

"I been fired from my last two jobs,
'Cause I don't take orders well,
'Specially from bosses who try to push me;
I just tell them to 'go to hell'.
My last girlfriend wanted me
To get an I-phone and wear a tie
Sometimes to a fancy restaurant,
I said I would when pigs fly.

"I went to 'Nam way back then,
Did my duty, got a tattoo or two,
Worked oil rigs and cowhand jobs;
Lots of women I could turn to,
But I been thinkin' I might
Need to change a little though,
Bend a little, give in a little,
Give up tryin' to be so damn macho."

May of 1945

I found the old newspaper
In the jar, crumbling, yellowed,
Where my Dad left it
In May of 1945.

I was 9 years old then,
We lived on a ranch
In southern Oklahoma
Back in May of 1945.

I remember the day
Like it was yesterday,
A gentle breeze blew
Up from the south.

Grass and trees were green,
Prairie flowers in bloom,
Quiet, calm, peaceful
In our tranquil world.

We'd been working cattle,
My job close the gate,
Stay out of the way,
Don't let 'em run back.

We brought the mail
To the ranchhouse that day
From the rural mailbox
On the way to the noon meal.

Dad unfolded the paper,
Grim, solemn, somber,
Put it on the kitchen table
For all of us to see.

First pictures of the horrors,
Starved, emaciated, naked bodies,
Piles of dead skeleton-like bodies,
Black-and-white photos.

Belsen, Buchenwald, Dachau,
Strange names, death camps,
Nowadays scenes all too familiar,
But the first ones then.

Stories and images
From the atrocity camps,
Hard to believe
What had been seen and heard.

Survivors staggered about in rags,
"Never Again," the headline blared,
"Buy War Bonds" printed
Across photos of fields of death.

"Here's what humans can do,"
Dad said, staring at the stark
Awful scenes of dead and dying.
"Don't forget it."

Looking back over the years,
I still remember the horror;
Dad put the paper in a jar,
Closed the lid, put it away.

The black-and-white images
Had burned into our souls,
"Don't forget it.
"Don't forget it."

The old newspaper
Brought it all back:
Dread and evil touched us
In May of 1945.

Momma and the Shack

Momma didn't like our old shack,
Tumbled-down and run-down,
Peelin' paint, windows that rattled,
Far away from any town.

Water well down the hill,
Outhouse farther still,
Wind whistlin' through the cracks;
Summer heat and winter chill.

Kitchen pans and coffee cans,
And a bucket or two,
To catch the drippin' leaks
When rains came through.

We'd roll up the mattresses,
Put the lamps where it was dry,
And huddle in the gloom,
Waitin' for storms to pass by.

Daddy was a rodeo man,
Often gone out on the road,
Leavin' Momma and us kids
To carry on a heavy load.

Me and sister and little brother
Did the best that we could,
To milk the cows, feed the chickens,
Chop and bring in the firewood.

Momma was always smilin'.
Sayin' we had to "make do,"
Even when the goin' was rough
And the pleasures were few.

She'd say that some future day
We wouldn't live in a shack,
We'd live high up on a hill,
And laugh when lookin' back

At the shabby squalid house,
The days of dusty poverty,
And remember the good times
When we dreamed of what might be.

Momma and the shack are gone,
But she was right to say
That we'd recall it all
With special fondness some day.

Money

Ain't it funny
What they say
About money?

Lovin' it's the root
Of an evil tree
Bearin' bitter fruit.

Could the culprit
Really be
The lack of it?

My Little Pony

My little pony
Knew the way
Back to the barn,
Though we might stray
Far and wide all around
The old neighborhood,
Over hill and valley,
Pasture, field and wood.

I could just
Let the reins go
And my pony would,
In those days long ago,
Take me home,
Safe and secure,
Findin' his way
Confident and sure.

The years have flown,
Now I'm far away
In a strange land,
Driftin' night and day,
Wishin' my little pony
Could take me home,
Back to the barn
Where I'd never roam.

My People's Music

My people, and my people's music,
Came from the hills, hollers and valleys
Of Georgia, Alabama and Arkansas,
Movin' to the plains of Oklahoma and Texas
In time for the Depression and the Dust Bowl.

Sharecroppers, tenant farmers, workin' timber,
Cotton mills, oil rigs, minimum wage;
Music helped lighten the burdens,
Honky-tonks, beer joints and oldtime tunes,
"Nine Pound Hammer" and "Roughneck Blues."

Rock-bottom poverty a way of life,
Fiddles, guitars, french harps, banjos,
Singin' in the fields and the churches,
Songs that spoke to their hearts,
Their souls, their hardscrabble existence.

Extended family, dirt poor, death and sorrow;
A girl about 13 died in a house fire,
A younger one gone with brain tumor,
Fiddle-playing son wrote hot checks,
Perished in the Arkansas State Prison.

But happiness, too, in close-knit families,
Raisin' kids and dogs and crops and gardens,
Huntin' and fishin', livin' close to the land,
Woods, streams, prairies wide and church on Sunday,
"Will the Circle Be Unbroken?" and "Amazing Grace."

Uncles and cousins and distant kin,
Answerin' the call when war came;
One shot in both legs at Normandy,
Another three years in a prison camp:
"Dear John", "Fraulein" and "Smoke on the Water."

And the music helped ease their inner core;
Country music was about them,
Their heartaches, their joys, their losses,
Their ups and downs, their lives,
Simple, raw, clear as a mountain stream.

Melodies and lyrics not complicated,
Easy to play and easy to understand;
No obscure, murky, perplexing
References, meanings, implications –
Words as sharp as a barb wire fence.

"You Are My Sunshine" and "Lovesick Blues,"
"Keep on the Sunny Side" and "Faded Love,"
Some sad songs, yearning for home and the past,
But laughing and light-hearted, too,
"Jambalaya" and "Pistol Packin' Mama."

Workin' people, workin' poor, hangin' on,
From the hard southern crucible,
Stoic, blue-collar, roughnecks, truckers,
Coal miners, knowin' and singin'
"Sixteen Tons" and "Mule Skinner Blues."

Despite amplifiers, flashin' lights,
Smoke, screamin' singers blastin' on TV,
Country music still lives and thrives
Whenever "Take Me Home, Country Roads"
Or "Your Cheatin' Heart" is played.

Humble its roots, denigrated as "hillbilly,"
Resonating with "Cold, Cold Heart,"
"The Last Roundup" and "Folsom Prison Blues,"
Tellin' the story of hard-workin' people,
And tellin' the story of this nation.

Never to Be Again

In the hot July afternoon,
I began to nod and doze
On my cool and shady porch
In hushed and drowsy repose.

In my dream, I saw 'em
Comin' from the southside
Like a mile-long windin' serpent,
A steady movin' longhorn tide.

Longhorns red, brown, smoky dun,
Whites and blacks and blues,
Light and dark and motley speckled,
Dappled in many hues.

Tough and hard to handle,
Long legs and big horns,
Wild from the Texas brush
Sharper'n cactus thorns.

Up from down deep in Texas,
'Cross the Brazos and the Red,
Flowin' over the rollin' hills,
A herd of three-thousand head.

In my reverie, they passed on by,
Cowboys ridin' flank and in back,
Swing and point and headed north,
Skirtin' the thickets and the blackjack.

Big hats, chaps and spurs,
Bandanas, boots and six-gun,
Ropes and saddles and dust,
And horses ready to run.

"You won't see our likes again,"
The cowboys called to me,
"We're takin' this herd to Abilene,
We're the last there'll ever be.

"No matter what's on ahead –
Storm, rain, wind or hail,
Stampede, rustlers or floodin' rivers –
This is the final drive up the trail."

In my dozin' driftin' state,
I watched 'em ridin' high,
Free-spirited, hell for leather,
'Neath the wide archin' sky.

Relentless, stoic and steady,
Lovin' freedom and liberty,
Get 'er done, stay the course,
No matter what the destiny.

"You won't see our likes again,"
The words slowly faded away
As longhorns and cowboys vanished
On that hot July day.

No Cure for Stupid

I tried to ride the bronc
That nobody could ride,
I shoulda knowed better,
I landed on my backside.

I challenged Big Dave
In the honky tonk parkin' lot,
I shoulda knowed better,
A black eye was what I got.

I tried my luck at the casino,
Bet my pay check on the dice,
I shoulda knowed better,
I let it ride, paid the price.

There ain't no cure for stupid,
That's what I've been told,
I've learned that's true no matter
If you're young, or if you're old.

No Place Like Home

Will we ever see bluebonnets again?
Or the blaze of Indian paint red?
Or the great domed archin' sky
Stretchin' away, clouds overhead?

We're stuck in this cursed place
Cold and cold wind, frost and snow
All around, frigid and shiverin',
Deep in your bones, twenty below.

I fear we'll never make it back
Where the cactus and mesquites grow –
Where the streams are crystal clear
And the sunsets are all aglow.

We wandered, restless on the move,
Always driftin', seekin' somethin' new,
And this is where we ended up –
Miles and miles of bleak and dismal view.

The story is an old one, I guess,
Told by restless souls who roam,
They never learn, they never learn –
There's absolutely no place like home.

O.W. Wheeler,
First Up the Trail

In 1867, O.W. Wheeler
With partners, Hicks and Wilson,
Made the first big cattle drive
All the way under summer sun
From deep in south Texas
To the loadin' pens in Abilene,
Bringin' 2400 head of longhorns,
A feat never before seen.

They broke out the Chisholm Trail,
Crossin' rivers – the Brazos and the Red,
The Cimarron and the Arkansas,
The first to follow the wagon tread
That Jesse Chisholm laid down
Some years before on the prairie –
The cattle road that soon became
Crowded with herds movin' freely.

History from then is sketchy,
Reports of what happened are few,
But apparently Wheeler bought
The cattle and hired drovers, too,
It was said he had 50 cowboys,
Four times the size of a normal crew,
Armed with six-shooters and rifles
To face any trouble they ran into.

The American cowboy myth
Was born on the trail that year,
When Wheeler and the longhorns
Made the drive along the frontier;
Cowboy boots and cowboy hat,
Spurs and ropes and well-worn saddle,
Pushin' into the Kansas cowtown,
Drovers, horses and big-horned cattle.

Reports say he bought 'em
For $10 a head near San Antone,
Sold 'em for $40 each in Abilene,
Total profits big, details unknown.
Word spread fast like wildfire
Around the ranches in Texas country,
Lots of money could be made,
Get 'em up there, do it quickly.

Oliver Walcott Wheeler,
Born in 1830 in Connecticut state,
Became a cattle trader and drover,
Before he helped to create
The American cowboy legend,
The great western icon and folk hero,
Which sprang from the trail drives;
He died in 1890 up in Idaho.

Okies Headed
For California

My aunt and uncle and their kids
Hugged my folks and us goodbye,
Climbed into the old model A truck,
Loaded with mattresses, wash tubs,
Bedsteads, chairs, tables, clothes,
Kitchenware, boxes tied with ropes,
Waterbags hanging on the front.

They left down the sandy lane,
Cousins in back, feet sticking out,
Holding to the tail gate railing;
We ran along behind in the sand.

The groaning, creaking old Ford,
Slowly moved away, leaving us behind,
Kicking up a cloud of red dirt dust;
The dust settled back down on us;
They turned at the Stringtown gravel road,
And moved out of sight,
Creeping up the hill to the west.

We waved as long as we could see them,
Then turned and walked
Through the falling dusty powder
Back to the old house.

Oklahoma October

Why can't October
Last all year long?
When a cooler sun
Is not as strong –

When winter's cold
Is far away,
And spring storms
Are held at bay –

When days shorten,
And cottonwood leaves
Begin to turn,
Float on the breeze –

When calm stillness
Fills the air,
And October's quietness
Spreads everywhere –

When things dial back
Under mild control,
And tranquility
Soothes the soul.

Old Corral

I rode my pony down the ridge
Into the valley below,
Crossed the creek, through the trees
Where the ranch house stood years ago.

Weeds, brush, plum thickets grow,
Barns, outbuildings all gone,
Empty, silent, abandoned, forlorn,
Nothin' left but foundation stone.

Then, posts from the old corral
Farther down the hill,
Leanin', fallin', but hangin' on,
Railin's, loadin' chute intact still.

Sunflowers fill the corral ground
Where we first tried our hand
At ropin', ridin', playin' cowboy,
Markin' calves with a smokin' brand.

Where I learned you get back on
After you'd been throwed,
To pull the cinches tight,
And carry your end of the load.

I was glad something remained
And to feel again the restless wind
That whistled through the cottonwoods,
Like meetin' an old long lost friend.

Clouds hung low, gray and dismal;
I looked with my memory's eye
At the collapsed, decayin' scene,
Saw the past, the past gone by.

I said farewell to another time,
Turned my pony and rode away,
Not lookin' back, and leavin' there
The old corral and thoughts of yesterday.

Old Friends

Old friends,
In my soul and in my heart,
Some are gone now,
But the memories
Like polished stones
Plucked from the river of life,
Remain to be savored
Recalled and cherished.

Some are here still
Making memories,
Filling the storehouse
Of my mind
With rememberances
To be collected,
Treasured and held
Like the polished stones

One-Night Rodeo

On a trail drive headed north,
Jake rode into old Fort Worth,
Lost his heart, don't you know,
In a wild one-night rodeo.

She was a dark-haired beauty,
Flashin' eye, black as the sea,
Dancin' and whirlin' across the floor,
Left Jake breathless, wantin' more.

She said she loved him dearly,
And vowed she'd be his only –
That it was love at first sight,
That he filled her with delight.

He pined for her all the way
To Kansas, waitin' for the day
He'd return for another go
At a wild one-night rodeo.

He yearned to make her his bride,
Take her to his ranch just outside
Goliad town, deep in the heart
Of Texas where they'd never part.

But it was never meant to be,
'Cause she was gone, you see,
When he came back from Abilene,
Searchin' for his dark-haired queen.

The local paper showed her photo,
Beamin', lookin' prim and all aglow,
She had married a wealthy banker,
And Jake was left with bitter anger.

He often remembers and dreams
More than he should, it seems,
About that time long ago
And the wild one-night rodeo.

Pioneer Cemetery

Tombstones leanin', weathered,
Scattered down the hill
Under the willows, cottonwoods,
In summer heat and winter chill.

November's frost fills the air,
Leaves rustle with the breeze,
Pass through neglected paths
Beneath barren empty trees.

I walk and pause and wonder,
The silence all around me,
The old pioneer cemetery
Left from days that used to be.

The names are hard to read,
Settlers who first worked the land,
Forgotten now in the rush of time,
Farmer, rancher wife, hired hand.

With wagons, horses, cows and plows,
They made the lottery and the run,
Diggin', pushin', pullin', toilin,'
Plantin' roots in the Oklahoma sun.

Wind howls along the ridge
Beneath a bleak gray sky;
Their journey ended here
In the graves where they lie.

Up from Texas, down from Kansas
And from the east and west,
They came to the lonely prairie,
Made a life, did their best.

Left a land much changed now,
Cities, towns, farms galore,
Their legacy all around us,
To remember forevermore.

Place Called "Home"

Why do I live way out here,
You keep asking me:
Why do I live where there's
No mountain greenery,
No seashore scenery –

Where it's dusty and bleak,
Where the wind blows,
Where it's dismal and flat,
And cactus grows
And water seldom flows –

The only answer I can give
To shed some light,
That might make sense –
The sun is bright –
And it feels right –

Dreary tho' it might be
'Neath the sky's arching dome,
One word explains it all –
After I wander and roam,
It's a place called "home."

Points to Ponder

Alpaca questions:
What do they call castrated alpacas?
Are they steers or geldings or what?
And do alpaca cowboys
Feast on alpaca mountain oysters?
And if not – why not?

Rain in August

Rain in August
On brown, dry, thirsty
Pastures and fields,

Good for the grass,
Good for the creeks and ponds,
Good for the winter wheat,

Good for the bluestem hay;
Maybe another cuttin',
Maybe a break-even year –

Rumble of thunder,
Flash of lightnin',
Raindrops on barn roof –

Chasin' the parchness,
Soothin' the baked prairie,
Green comin' back

To break the dry
And arid grip
Of summer heat;

Watch it splashin',
Cheery, gleeful,
Bringin' hope once more;

Cattle driftin',
Grazin' and watered
Into the trees,

Spirits are raised,
Sunny the smiles
On farm and ranch

Way out here
On the drought-kissed
Southern Plains –

Relish and rejoice,
Nothin' can replace
Rain in August.

Rain

The rain falls pitter-patter
On my roof, shrubs and yard;
Raindrops drift down my windowpane –
They don't go back up again.

The drops plop like little bombs
In the puddles under my red oak tree,
And they aren't going back up
Into the clouds from whence they came.

The rain falls and falls,
And time moves on and on,
And you can't call the raindrops back,
And you can't erase what time has done.

And when the bell is rung,
You can't unring it –
And when the bullet leaves the gun,
You can't make it go back again.

And you can't make what is past
Be unrung and undone;
You can't change it back again,
But you can carry it with you always.

Rememberin'

I remember
Another December
When winds blew cold,
Skies were dismal gray,
Trees had lost their leaves
On that melancholy day.

The auction drew
Quite a few;
The spread had seen its last,
The old Circle R was through;
They sold the horses
And all the cattle, too.

I said farewell,
Wished them well;
Cowhand jobs were hard to find
Tho' I tried and tried to land one;
The range was gettin' smaller,
And my saddle days were done.

I went down
Into the town
And took a factory job
So's to make ends meet;
Now I do my ridin'
Down a city street.

Dear to me
Is my memory,
Checkin' fences way out there,
The canyons, hills and streams,
Seein' sunrise and sunsets
Now only in my dreams.

Restless wind
Without end;
Sleepin' with the herd,
Sun and sleet, ice and snow,
Workin', brandin' and roundups,
Watchin' 'em graze and grow.

This December
I remember
When I was a cowboy
And lived the cowboy way,
Close to nature out-of-doors
Before it all went away.

Rich and Famous

The leader of the town,
A man of wide renown,
Rich and famous as can be,
Was elected naturally
'Cause he had plenty
Of fame and money.

The people didn't care
That almost everywhere
Problems popped up galore,
Troubles sprouted by the score,
City funds disappeared
While they clapped and cheered.

He was famous, don't you see?
Rich and famous as can be.
What he was famous for
Nobody really knew, nor
Did they ask about that stuff
'Cause famous was good enough.

Robot Cowboys

"Robots are everywhere,"
Shorty says to Billy Bob,
"They're takin' over,
Doin' every kind of job.

"I saw this tee-vee show
How they're makin' cars,
Playin' chess and ping pong
And bartendin' in bars.

"They chop up chickens,
Cut and harvest crops –
They're used in storerooms,
Handy with brooms and mops.

"They can mow yards,
Dismantle bombs and stuff –
Fight fires and other things
When the goin' gets tough.

"They're composin' songs,
Cookin' fancy meals –
Doin' it better'n humans,
The research reveals.

"They're drivin' tractors,
Fillin' prescription drugs;
They're tellers in banks
And shampooin' rugs.

"Servin' up fast food,
Dealin' cards in Vegas –
Real good for bidness,
No perks and no wages.

"They say them robots
Have artificial intelligence –
They're a lot smarter'n us,
They got super-super sense.

"Experts say automation
Is comin' fast, of course,
And will take the place
Of many in the workforce.

"Robots will control the world,
Some people are sayin',
And replace the human race
At workin' and playin'."

Billy Bob shakes his head,
"If they're really smart,
They won't become cowhands –
Be too dumb on their part.

"We'll be safe, I'm sure;
The cowboy occupation
They'll leave to us dummies –
Even if they rule the nation."

Rodeo Bum

I'm a rodeo bum, he said,
There's always another town –
It seems just like a curse,
This driftin' up and down.

I got a rovin', rovin' spirit
That keeps me travelin' on,
That drives me, haunts me,
Makes me drift and drift alone.

I shoulda settled down,
Stopped bein' a rollin' stone,
Tumblin' like a tumbleweed –
The rodeo road's my home.

I've had it in my soul forever,
This affliction that's got aholda me:
Keep movin' on and movin' on,
See what the next thing might be.

Cheap motels and greasy spoons,
Drivin' down the old highway,
Tryin' to make it to the next one,
Rovin' restless night and day.

There ain't no cure, they say,
'Til injury, the grave or old age
Puts an end to this trip of mine,
And closes out my final page.

Rompin' Roy: Cowboy Elf

Rompin' Roy wore his boots,
Janglin' spurs, wide-brimmed hat,
And all the other elves
Really didn't cotton to that.

Roy was too loud, stompin'
Around Santa's workshop
In his Levis, red bandana,
Twirlin' his lasso non-stop.

Santa warned him once or twice
That he should get to work
With the other elves makin' toys,
Stop bein' a cowboy jerk.

Roy wore his big belt buckle,
Bragged about bein' a hand
Way down on a reindeer ranch
In a distant wintry land.

All the elves rolled their eyes,
And scoffed at his tales
Of ridin' and drivin' herds
All along the reindeer trails.

"Roy, stop actin' like a fool,"
They would sneer and say,
"You're keepin' us from gettin'
Things ready for Christmas Day."

Roy would sing cowboy songs,
Try to rope and ride the reindeer
In the barn and the feedlot
At almost any time of year.

It was a stormy Christmas Eve,
Santa was loadin' up the sleigh,
When a freakish clap of thunder
Brought sudden shock and dismay.

The reindeer panicked and ran,
A good old-fashioned stampede,
Dancer and Vixen and Rudolph, too,
Whole herd runnin' full-speed.

They charged across the snow,
Right around the North Pole,
Comet and Cupid and Donner,
Runnin' wild, out of control.

Santa didn't know what to do;
That's when Rompin' Roy,
Ridin' and spurrin' a reindeer,
Like a real old-time cowboy,

Came outta the barn full blast,
Streakin' hard for the lead,
Gettin' in front and turnin' 'em,
Stoppin' the reindeer stampede.

He got 'em millin' in a circle
And halted the frantic runaway,
Moved 'em calmly and carefully
Back to Santa's sleigh.

All the elves were amazed
At the skill Roy showed;
They were happy and hilarious
Readyin' the sleigh's heavy load.

Now they're singin' Roy's praises –
And that's how it came to be
That they're wearin' Western garb,
Whoopin' it up with cowboy glee.

So all around the North Pole
The elves, and even Santa himself,
Are smitten and delighted
With Rompin' Roy, the cowboy elf.

Root Cause
Of Most Trouble

The old cowboy leaned on the bar,
Pushed back his hat, sez to me:
"Son, I've seen some bad things
In my day, bad as they can be.

"Floods, fires, grass-killin' droughts,
Destruction left after a tornado
Tears through a homestead and a town;
Nature's fury, don't you know?

"But it appears to me the baddest
Things are what humans carry out;
They lie, cheat, steal, break all the rules,
In my view, they're the worst, no doubt.

"The Ten Commandments are broken to bits,
And the seven deadly sins, I must say,
Are some of the most popular activities
Takin' place every day in every way.

"I have concluded after much thought
That the primary root of all this mayhem
Stems from the fact that human bein's
Are filled plumb up to the very brim

"With a restless notion to flounder about,
To scurry and scamper up and down,
Fitful, agitated, never at ease or content,
Always pushin' and movin' around.

"Tryin' to fix things what ain't broke,
They can't leave well enough alone,
Never satisfied with how things are,
Wantin' change, results unknown.

"They can't stay on their own range,
Accept their lot, be happy at home;
They just can't remain still and quiet,
And resist the constant urge to roam.

"The grass is always greener, it seems,
On the other side of the fence,
And that's the basic reason, I opine,
Behind most trouble, outrage and offense."

Sale Barn Saga

Pickup trucks and cattle trailers,
Goosenecks and bumper pull,
Clustered 'round the sale barn,
Parkin' lot almost full.

Battered and dented and showin'
Signs and scars of haulin' loads
Up and down and all around
Dusty, rutted country roads.

'Cause it's sale day today,
Farmers and ranchers comin' in
To buy some or sell some,
Or see how the biddin's been.

Pens out behind the barn
Packed with heifers, springers, culls,
Mama cows with calves,
Feeders, canners, steers and bulls.

Movin' 'em from pen to pen,
Cattle prods and cow manure,
Taggin', loadin', bawlin' yearlin's,
Livestock sale, that's for sure.

Buyers and sellers and lookers,
Scattered around the arena stands,
Scruffy boots and work shirts,
Sun-beaten faces, calloused hands.

Feed store caps, cowboy hats,
Chaps and spurs on a few,
No glitz or rhinestones here,
Only workin' cowhands in view.

Crack of a whip, cattle crowded
Through the gate, into the ring,
Auctioneer chant, sellin' hard:
How much will they bring?

Bidders quietly makin' signs –
Nod of the head, thumb in the air,
Lifted finger to show all right,
We'll take the ones in there.

Those that sell are rushed out
To be loaded and shipped away,
And buyin' and sellin' goes on
Throughout the busy day.

"We was hopin' for a little more,
But that'll have to do;
We had to sell the calf crop
To make it another year or two."

The sale barn drama unfolds;
It's where the real cowboys see
What they can buy and sell,
And what the bottom line will be.

Shade of Their Skin

The trail boss was hirin'
Cowhands seasoned and green
To take a longhorn herd
All the way to Abilene:

"And I don't care 'bout
The shade of their skin,
Or the lingo they speak,
Or scrapes they've been in –

"Or if they wore
The blue or the gray,
Or how they come to be
Driftin' down this way.

"I don't give a hoot,
And I don't need to know,
If they come from shanty town
Or from silk-stockin' row.

"Can they rope
And can they ride?
Can they stick it out –
Are they tough as rawhide?

"Can they hold the herd
On a dark and stormy night?
Can they get 'em movin'
At first break of daylight?

"Can they swim 'em
'Cross the river flood,
Past deadly quicksand,
Mire, muck and mud?

"Can they turn 'em
When they're off and runnin'?
Can they stand their ground
When raiders come gunnin'?

"Can they keep on keepin' on
Over the dry, burnin' plain?
Can they hold 'em fast
Through hail, wind and rain?

"Can they wrangle
The broncs half-broke?
Can they push 'em
Through brush and scrub oak?

"Can they stay in the saddle,
Sleep on the ground,
With howlin' wind
And lightnin' all around?

"Are they handy with
A brandin' iron or six-gun?
Can they keep ridin' despite
Icy wind or blazin' sun?

"And I don't care
A bubble or a squeak
What they look like
Or the lingo they speak.

"It don't matter,
Let me say again,
Where they're from
Or the shade of their skin."

Sharecropper Boy

When he was a sharecropper's boy,
He first felt the bite of wanderlust,
Down those long, long cotton rows
Pullin' a cotton sack through the dust.

He knew he had to go aroamin',
Wanderin', rovin', to the world beyond
Away from the red-dirt fields,
Feel the freedom of the vagabond.

So on the open road he went,
Driftin' from place to place,
Always on the go, not settlin' down,
Sun and rain upon his face.

But despite all the years,
He never lost across his back,
The weight, heavy tug, the pull
Of the strap of the cotton sack.

It followed and followed wherever
He went no matter what he did,
Cities and towns and battles won,
He remained a sharecropper's kid.

It's really true what they say:
You can't take the country
Outta the boy, try as you might,
'Cause raisin' does shape identity.

But pulled from those dusty fields
Came perseverance, hope for the best,
Willingness to work, stoic and steady,
And strength when hard-pressed.

Skeeters

"The skeeters are bad right now,"
Billy Bob says to his pal Shorty,
"But they ain't as bad as they was
Down on the Brazos recently.

"They was so thick they blotted
Out the sun – makin' it dark as night,
All the birds quit flyin' about,
Nested in trees, waitin' for daylight."

"Well," Shorty says, "that ain't nothin'.
Our chuckwagon was stuck in quicksand
On the Cimarron – we couldn't get it out,
And skeeters were big as your hand.

"We roped a passel of 'em together,
Tied 'em tight to the old chuckwagon,
Shooed 'em, and they pulled it out
Up the bank, a slick son of a gun."

Billy Bob shook his head, grinned,
"I think that under any circumstance,
That old sayin' is always true:
The first liar ain't got a chance."

Something About Time

I came to the deserted crossroads
Where once stood the old country store,
The two-room school, the little white church,
All gone now through time's door.

Weeds and brush and sunflowers
Grow where the community gathered
In times gone by, gone to the past,
Faded away, drifted and scattered.

I pondered why I had stopped
And wondered about the runaway
Dash of time's onward rush
From then to the present day.

Time marches on, does not wait,
Philosophers spin their theories,
And we're left when it has passed
With the remains of our memories.

There's something about time –
The best medicine, eases sorrow –
Time flies, the greatest healer,
Always moving toward tomorrow.

Somethin's Tryin'
To Kill You

Billy Bob and Shorty
Was workin' out on the Caprock,
Livin' in a rundown line shack,
Fixin' fence, herdin' Circle R stock.

One day Shorty sez to Billy Bob:
"I been readin' this here magazine
'Bout how where you live helps
Make you nice or rattlesnake mean.

"If you live in the mountains
Then you're liable to be an introvert –
And if you live in a big city,
You might tend to be an extrovert.

"Seein' trees and lots of green stuff
Lowers blood pressure for you,
Lulls you into bein' cheered up,
So's you don't bite nails in two.

"Where it's dark and gloomy all the time,
You might be filled with sorrow,
Needin' some sunshine to keep you
From feelin' like there's no tomorrow.

"Too much heat makes you irritable,
Angry and kicks up the crime rate –
Too much cold can cause the blues
And make you curse your fate.

"Livin' in the woods might make you
Peaceful, calm and easy-goin',
But you might become a bit suicidal
Where the wind's always blowin'."

Billy Bob stops him right there:
"But, Shorty, out here we got mesquite,
Cactus, snakes, lizards and howlin' wind –
Too many icy blasts, too much scorchin' heat.

"Out here you don't need to be suicidal –
You can count on it pert nigh always,
With wild broncs, bulls and twisters, too,
Somethin's tryin' to kill you most days."

Starin' at Purty Girls

The old man sat on the porch,
A black patch coverin' one eye –
His grandson, just turned six,
Played on the swing nearby.

The boy stared up at the patch,
"Grandpa, what happened to your eye?"
The boy asked with concern,
Waited for the old man's reply.

"I lost it lookin' at purty girls.
I plumb wore it out starin' when
All the girls were strollin' by;
I kept starin' again and again.

"And that's what'll happen to you
If you're gawkin' and gawkin'
At all the purty girls too much –
You'd best to just keep on walkin'."

"But Grandpa, I don't like 'em,"
The boy said with surprise.
"I sure ain't lookin' at 'em –
They won't do nothin' to my eyes!"

"Just wait," the old man said,
"Someday in this old world,
You'll find you can't keep
From starin' at some purty girl.

"And you'll lose more'n an eye –
You'll lose your heart, too.
You'll be struck down by love,
With luck, that'll happen to you!"

Summer Heat

Summer heat comes early
To the southern plains,
And stays and stays –
Hot winds and no rains.

Ponds and creeks dry up,
Sun a flamin' ball of fire,
Mercury readin' keeps
Goin' higher and higher.

"Hot enough for ya yet?"
A common form of greetin'
Whenever inhabitants here
Happen to be meetin'.

Sizzlin', swelterin', scorchin',
Broilin', boilin', burnin',
When, oh when will cool
October be returnin'?

Superheroes

Superman leaps tall buildings,
Spiderman spins and spins,
Batman in his batmobile,
And Captain Marvel always wins.

Green Arrow and Green Lantern
Green as they could be,
Plastic Man reachin' out
Catchin' baddies easily –

And there's Wonder Woman
With bracelets and lasso,
Even the Swamp Thing,
A wet and spongy hero.

There were many such heroes
During my childhood days,
When I devoured comic books,
Movie serials and radio plays.

But the greatest of them all
Throughout our fair land,
Was the one on horseback,
The hard-ridin' cowhand.

Sweetest Sounds

I like to hear the sound, he said,
Of a rooster at daybreak,
A distant owl faintly hootin'
When you're just comin' awake –

A coyote howlin' way out yonder,
And mamma cows bawlin'
For their babies at twilight,
As a gentle rain is fallin' –

The muffled clop of horsehoof
Ridin' along a dusty trail
Through the prairie grassland,
Evenin' shadows dim and pale –

Wind rufflin' through the oaks,
A dog barkin' far away,
Water ripplin' in a creek,
Crickets at close of day –

The pony's bridle jinglin',
The creakin' of the saddle,
Down the hill toward the barn,
The lowin' of the cattle –

But the sweetest sound, he said,
Is my woman hummin' softly,
Singin' a tender, tender song
That's just for me, just for me.

Texas and the Big Bang

The old West Texas cowboy,
In town for the rodeo,
Wandered into the lecture hall
And sat on the very first row.

He listened as the speaker,
An astronomer of world renown,
With charts and graphs aplenty
Gave the astrophysics rundown.

The old cowboy raised his hand,
And in his West Texas drawl,
Asked if he'd heard it right,
Did he understand it all?

"Everything was squished to a pin,
All squeezed into a teeny, tiny dot –
The sun, the moon, the earth,
The stars all in one little spot?"

"That's right," the speaker said,
"One microscopic singularity,
Which exploded and that's how
The Big Bang came to be."

"Even Texas, too?" the cowboy asked.
"That's exactly right," was the reply.
"Everything in the universe exploded out,
Everything we see in the earth and sky."

"You mean," the cowboy asked,
"From Texarkana plumb to El Paso
Was part of that tiny little dot,
Everything from Houston to Amarillo?

"All the cows and people, too?
The mountains and the prairie,
The rivers, creeks and streams,
Every blade of grass, every tree?"

"That's correct," the astronomer said.
"Every atom and molecule and electron.
Everything in the entire universe,
Every single proton and neutron."

The old cowboy shook his head,
"You just plain gotta be funnin' me,
Texas would never be a tiny little dot –
New York City or New Jersey, maybe."

Things Gone
Or Goin' Away

Drive-in movies, buggy whips
ain't been in style
for a while –

8-track tapes, 5-cent cigars
have faded away
like yesterday –

Tail fins and Studebakers
from days of yore
are no more –

Soda fountains and Edsels,
few and far between
rarely ever seen –

And hand-written letters
nobody sends
to their friends –

Small family farms
just about gone,
a few hangin' on –

And another thing goin' –
the workin' cowhand
ain't in demand –

And when he's gone –
the world'll be
shrunken severely –

Those Were the Days,
The Good Old Days

Sloppin' the pigs,
watchin' 'em wallow
in the mud and muck;
choppin' wood
for the pot-bellied stove
when the north wind blows;
walkin' two miles
to the two-room school –
"Those were the days,
the good old days."

Carryin' firewood
from the wood pile,
stackin' it behind
the red glowin' stove;
bugs, spiders, sometimes scorpions
crawlin' out on the floor;
wind howlin' outside
through the cracks,
"Those were the days,
the good old days."

Hoein' cotton, pullin' bolls
when its 110 in the shade,
weedin' the garden in the sun,
pickin' beans, black-eyed peas,
tomatoes off the vine,
cannin' cookers runnin' all summer,
peelin', slicin', cuttin',
shellin', hours on end –
"Those were the days,
the good old days."

Milkin' cows by hand
at dawn and dusk,
turnin' the cream separator;
pumpin' water at the well,
totin' it to the house,
two buckets at a time,
heatin' on coal-oil cookstove
for cookin', cleanin', washin' –
"Those were the days,
the good old days."

Breakin' ice on the pond,
haulin' hay to the cows
when snow is on the ground;
fixin' fence, diggin' post holes,
ground hard as concrete,
stretchin' wire, pullin' calves,
brandin', dehornin', doctorin' –
"Those were the days,
the good old days."

An hour to get to town,
rattlin' old pickup creepin' along,
deep, deep ruts,
road sticky red-dirt mud,
more often blowin' dust;
feed sack shirts, feed sack dresses,
homemade and homespun,
patched and patched to "make do."
"Those were the days,
the good old days."

The outhouse down the hill,
feedin' chickens, gatherin' eggs,
plowin' the wheat field,
ridin' the Poppin' Johnny
round and round and round;
livin' on the edge of the old Dust Bowl
right below the poverty line –
"Those were the days,
the good old days."

When I pine and pine
for the days gone by –
when recallin' how it was,
when yearnin' to go back
to those distant times –
when nostalgia clouds my vision –
I remember the somber truth,
the stern cold reality back when
"Those were the days,
the good old days."

Time to Ponder

Summer's end winding down,
The sun sets behind the hill;
On the porch, weathered house,
I sit and listen, quiet and still.

The vast prairie spreads all around
In the purple evening twilight;
A crow calls from the cedar tree
And day slowly fades to night.

The moon's golden globe hangs high,
Stars begin their twinkling show,
A time of recollection and reflection,
And to ponder life's ebb and flow.

My thoughts keep turning back
To the woods and fields and streams,
And the lessons I have learned
Of nature, creation and dreams.

Words and philosophies fail
When we try to capture the splendor
Of the world that surrounds
And fills us with awesome wonder.

Tracks Fadin' Away

Ruts from the wagon wheels
Are slowly fadin' away,
Hoofprints from the longhorns
Are barely visible today.

You've got to look hard
To see where the old trail
Ran from Texas up to Kansas;
Not much left to tell the tale.

Some signs remain, they say,
At crossin's like Red River Station,
Or Lookout Point or Caldwell,
Some seen only in your imagination.

The tracks are still there faintly
Around Bison, Renfrow, Yukon,
Belton and Round Rock in Texas,
But most of the old trail is gone.

Three-thousand head, wild longhorns,
Cowboys, horses and open country,
No fences, no towns, no highways,
Miles and miles, open and free.

They followed Jesse's old trail;
What a sight it must have been
To have seen the epic drives
That took place back then.

We can only bring to mind
Those days and their significance,
When their struggles gave birth
To cowboy myth and romance.

Trail to Abilene

On the trail to Abilene,
The wind's in the mesquite,
Whistles through the sage,
Blowin' through the heat.

The rivers are runnin' full
And the herd is hard to hold,
And way out on the plains,
Sunsets are fiery gold.

Listen for the coyote cries,
And the hauntin' nightbird calls;
Watch the driftin' prairie moon
As darkenin' nighttime falls.

Tryin' to sleep and get some rest,
Hopin', hopin' they don't run.
Afore they're out on the trail,
Another day -- hot, hot sun.

Drivin' em up from deep in Texas,
'Crossin' the Brazos and the Red,
Into the Territory, wilder'n wild,
Pushing on with 2,000 head.

Down off Monument Hill,
'Cross the flooded Washita,
Past the Cimarron quicksand,
Over the ragin' Arkansas.

One puncher left buried
In a shallow prairie grave;
He rode to turn the leaders,
Runnin' hard, young and brave.

Rustlers stampeded the herd,
Aimin' to get some cattle,
But the cowboys drove 'em off,
Spendin' the night in the saddle.

In the dance halls and saloons,
'Twas a wild and wooly scene,
When they finally drove the herd
Down the streets of Abilene.

On the trail to Abilene,
The ones who made the drive
Say they'll do it again –
If they make it back alive.

Trail to Nowhere

I ponder the gloomy night,
rain whispers against the window,
cowtown hotel creaks and groans,
and what do I have to show
for the years of my life
ridin' a trail to nowhere –
thoughts of those I've lost and wronged
and the awful ache of despair.

Broken promises, broken dreams,
tellin' myself once more,
Cowboy, can there be forgiveness?
can there be peace at the core?
followin' the whiskey road ahead,
they say I'll surely find
desolation and desperation,
regret, remorse and a troubled mind.

When they tally up my brand
and my last loop is thrown,
what will be the final count
when my earthly days have flown?
what tracks will I leave
from my careless ride?
what will be my legacy
when I cross the Great Divide?

Now the night and the past
press down smother and depress me,
fillin' me with pain and sorrow
and the torment of memory.
I need to find a new range,
change my ways to get there,
and leave the dust behind
on this trail to nowhere.

Trickle Down

Billy Bob and Shorty delivered
A load of Big Ben's steers
To the sale barn in Fort Worth,
Retired to a bar for Lone Star beers.

Billy Bob says to Shorty:
"What's this 'trickle down' theory
I keep hearin' about on TV?
Could you explain that to me?"

"Well," Shorty says,"'trickle down'
Means fixin' it so rich folks
Can make more and more money;
That'll help us poor cowpokes."

"You mean," Billy Bob says,
"Lettin' Big Ben get bigger and bigger
Will make all of us better off?
That'll make us all get richer?"

"Yep," Shorty says with a nod,
"He'll expand, buy more cows and hire
More cowboys, spend more dough
On land, fence posts and barb wire.

"So if he gets his expenses cut,
His taxes reduced way down low,
He'll have more to spread around,
Make the whole economy grow.

"And another thing he can do,
I'm really proud to say,
Is that with all that extra income,
He can raise our cowboy pay."

Billy Bob pondered this awhile,
Sipped his beer with a frown,
"But he just bought a plush condo
At the seaside in an Aruba town."

"Well," Shorty said, "if you look
At the big picture, you'll see
That when he bought that condo,
He did wonders for the Aruba economy."

Under the Peach Tree

Under the peach tree
at the end of the garden,
we buried Buster,
marked the grave with a rock;
no memorials or eulogies,
no fancy funeral procession,
no flags flyin' at half-staff,
just Mom, little brother and me.

I was ten and so was Buster;
my earliest memories –
climbin' on his back, pullin' his ears,
wrestlin' him on the grass
in the backyard
by the old willow tree.
He was a pup and so was I,
and we grew together.

Runnin' around the farm,
chasin' rabbits, diggin'
after prairie dogs and bullsnakes,
roamin' fields, pastures and woods,
helpin' bring in the cows
at milkin' time –
swimmin' in the farm ponds,
fishin' in the little creek.

Buster got older,
spent more time sleepin'
in his favorite cool spot
under the front porch.
That's where we found him
one hot day in August –
Buster had passed on
to the paradise for dogs.

No testimonials, no somber
mournful dirges;
the world kept on turnin',
really didn't notice –
but for me a melancholy
bleakness in my heart –
the day we buried Buster
under the peach tree.

Under the Stars

When I was a boy
On the farm,
On summer nights,
We'd sleep on blankets
Under the willows

In the backyard
And watch the stars
Wheel overhead,
Bright and sharp and clear –

And we'd dream
Of spaceships
And far away things
And happy trails –

Before the world
Came down on us.

Veterans Day

Veterans Day, flags, parade,
Those from World War Two are few,
More from Korea and Vietnam,
Some from Afghanistan and Iraq, too.

He went down with his cane,
Wore the old uniform,
Sergeant stripes, airborne patch,
Clear day sunny and warm.

When they saw the burns,
Some would look away,
And scars on his face
Made some uneasy that day.

Baghdad and Ramadi, too,
Flashed in his mind's eye,
The dust, the rubble, the dying;
Fires that lit up the sky.

Months in rehab to walk again,
Injuries outside, pain inside,
Booze and pills to finally adjust,
To live again, to put it aside.

"Thank you for your service, sir,"
They said as they passed,
And he nodded quietly,
Standin' tall and standin' fast.

He wore the medals, Purple Heart,
Pinned upon his chest,
And remembered all the buddies
Now asleep in eternal rest.

Some shook his hand and said,
"We had to fight 'em over there,"
As if they really understood,
"So we don't fight 'em over here.

"Thank you, sir, for what you did
To help keep us free;
They hate us, want to kill us,
'Cause we live in liberty."

Village

I live in a village;
Some call it a town,
Or even a small city
On its way down.

At the big chains,
Shoppers now meet;
Buildings are empty
Along main street.

Hostile to outsiders,
Scornful of change,
Folks stick close
To the old home range.

Church tribes flourish,
Kind to kind,
Nothing to disturb
The placid mind.

After the fires
Of life outside,
After roaming
Far and wide,

This is where
I drift along,
To find peace,
A soothing song.

Wallows

Round depressions dot the pasture,
Curious signs from a time gone by,
Where blue stem and native grasses grow,
Where Indian paint, black-eyed susans
And blue sage nod in the wind.

Prairie land never touched by the plow –
Where water stands after a rain –
The final proof and evidence
That countless buffalo
Once roamed across the grasslands.

Shaggy bison cows and bulls and calves
Wallowed out dusty places in the soil,
Fighting insects or cooling off
Or just because it felt good –
We'll probably never know.

Sixty million of the beasts once
Blanketed the plains, they say,
Now no great herds are on the move,
No bands of hunters following after –
The beasts and hunters have gone,
Leaving only the wallows.

Wanna be a Cowboy Blues

He's got the wanna be a cowboy blues,
And he's had it from an early age –
Horses, saddles, spurs and longhorn cattle –
Dreams of ridin' 'cross the purple sage.

His teachers said read Shakespeare,
He liked Zane Grey and the sagebrush sea;
He didn't care much for schoolin' –
'Twas a cowboy he wanted to be.

Roy and Gene and Hopalong, too,
Gallopin' up on the silver screen,
Doin' all the things he wanted to do –
Ridin' and ropin' scene after scene.

His Pop made him stop tryin' to rope
The calves and milk cows on the farm,
Told him to quit runnin' their old horse
' Afore he caused real damage and harm.

But now he's stuck in a traffic jam,
Trucks, cars, exhaust fumes all around;
Car horns, motors whinin', brakes squealin',
No coyotes howlin', no lone prairie sound.

Urban blight sprawls in every direction,
And he lives now in a gritty haze,
Pollution, congestion, crowds everywhere;
He longs for clear skies and cowboy days.

And he wants to be ridin' out west –
The wanna be blues comin' on strong –
Away from the big city squalor,
The frantic, hurried and hustlin' throng.

He'll never go back to the country,
The die is cast now he fears –
He's trapped far from his prairie home,
Livin' out his final days and years.

Water Moccasin

I was cane-pole fishin',
Rock Creek dreamin',
watchin' my bobber
float on the water –
restin' in the shade
of the pecan trees –

When not 10 feet away,
my reverie broken,
rustlin' in the leaves,
a water moccasin,
a cottonmouth slithered
down the bank –

Long and dark and venomous,
scaly faint bluish brown
and yellowish bands –
I froze, startled;
it paused slightly
before it went into the water,

Raised its triangle-shaped head,
seemed to look at me
with a cat-like eye,
then slip on its pale belly
into the creek,
slidin' silently away –

I got my cane pole,
my line and minnow bucket,
my water jug,
and quietly cautiously
left the fishin' hole
to the cottonmouth –

Where Have The "Westerns" Gone?

Have you noticed? They ain't makin'
Western movies much any more –
And the only cowboys on TV
Are in reruns we've seen before.

And "Western" is just about gone
From the country/western song –
And country music's more like
"Rock", which is definitely wrong.

Cowboy hats, boots and buckles
Are in style for some, it seems,
But not many real cowboys
Show up on TV or movie screens.

Remember when NBC stood for
"Nothin' But Cowboys" back then?
"Bonanza" and "Wagon Train"
Probably ain't comin' back again.

Marshal Dillon has left us,
John Wayne, Gene and Roy, too,
Have ridden off into the sunset –
Gone like the mornin' dew.

Cowboy songs like "Cattle Call"
Or "Ghost Riders in the Sky,"
Ain't on Top 10 lists these days;
They're missin' – don't ask why?

I guess cowboys are fadin' way
From our culture and that's a shame;
We still need the cowboy code,
The cowboy way, cowboy acclaim.

This complaint is an old one;
Nothin' stays the same, times change,
And you have to accept new things –
Even way out on the Western range.

The cowboy showed us how
To stand for what was right,
To be independent, loyal and brave,
No matter how tough the fight.

Tales of cowboys and the Old West
Are vanishin' from popular view –
Just when we need the legends
And myths to carry us through.

Where I'll Be

Martha Mae, Martha Mae,
Listen to what I say,
I'm gonna go down,
Roundup's in Goliad town;
I'm hirin' on,
Be gone at dawn
To take 'em north,
For what it's worth.
Please remember,
I'll return in September.

Martha Mae, Martha Mae,
Wait for me, I say,
I ain't too old,
Or so I'm told,
For one more drive;
This'll make five
Times I've seen
The trail to Abilene.
So don't you cry –
I'll see you bye and bye.

Martha Mae, Martha Mae,
I just can't stay away
From cowboyin' on the trail,
To hear the coyotes wail,
The wide, wide prairie,
The wind blowin' free,
The horses and the cattle,
Livin' in the saddle –
Hard it might be,

But it's the life for me.
I've got to go,
The dangers I know –
Stampede and flood,
River and quicksand mud,
Rustlers in the night,
Storms and snakebite,
Lightnin' and hail –
Perils of the trail –
But it calls me –
It's where I wanna be.

Martha Mae, Martha Mae,
You can visit me someday
At the Red River spot,
The lonely plot,
Where now I rest
Along the crest
Lookin' down the valley
'Neath the willow tree;
My final journey –
It's where I'll be.

Why So Many Stars?

Billy Bob and Shorty,
Night-herdin' on the Texas Caprock,
When Billy Bob says, lookin' up,
"Why do you suppose
The Good Lord made so many stars?"

"Well," Shorty says, "the preacher man
Says He did it for us.
So's we'd be impressed."

"Why, hell," Billy Bob says,
"I'd be impressed with a few dozen.
But they say there are millions –
Billions even. More than you can count.

"And while we're talkin',
Why do you suppose He made
These longhorns so ornery?
And why even make rattlers
And scorpions and flies at all?"

"Well," Shorty replies, "I guess
He did it all for us.
So's we'd be impressed."

"And I suppose," Billy Bob says,
"The twisters and the heat,
The prickly pear and miles of sand?
All for us, so's we'd be impressed?"

"You got it," Shorty says,
"Ain't you impressed yet?"

Winds of Many Kinds

Winds of many kinds
Swirl across the prairie,
Around my prairie home
Singin' constantly.

Sometimes fierce and strong,
Knockin' down fences,
Uprootin' trees, tearin' off roofs,
Batterin' our senses.

Howlin' and screamin',
Whistlin' outside
On dark rainy nights,
A wet stormy tide.

Sometimes from the south,
Hot gust after gust,
Dryin' out the country,
Scorchin', full of dust.

And wintry winds blowin',
Icy cold and chillin',
Sharp as a knife,
Leaf and bloom killin'.

Bringin' raw and bitter
Blasts of sleet and snow,
Whiteouts and blizzards,
Addin' to winter's woe.

Springtime often sees
Squall and gale,
Wind blowin' hard,
Downpour, flood and hail.

Summer doldrums fall,
Scarcely a breath of air,
The weathervane hangs
Motionless up there.

But it's a gentle wind,
A soft and coolin' breeze,
That I like the best
Rustlin' through the trees,

Whisperin', murmurin',
Swayin' the wavin' wheat,
Kissin' the noddin' flowers,
Lush and scented sweet.

Soothin' and calmin',
The peaceful wind,
Hummin' a melody
Like an old friend.

Winds of many kinds
Sweep on their way,
Touchin' our lives
Day after day.

You Ain't In New York Anymore

Yep, that's cow manure,
You need to get some boots,
Get rid of those Reeboks,
You don't need no fancy suits.

Get a real hat with a brim,
The way you looks a pity,
Lose that cap that sez,
"I Love New York City."

Loosen the reins just a bit,
The pony'll put 'em in the pen,
You just grip the saddle horn,
He's done it again and again.

That's the iron for brandin'
And it's glowin' red hot;
We gotta work these calves,
So crowd 'em in the cowlot.

Push 'em in the chute,
We got lotsa work to do,
Shut and lock the headgate
When the head pokes through.

Yep, just press that brand
Right high up on the hip,
It burns and singes a bit,
Hold it tight, don't let it slip.

Cowhands might get kicked
And butted a little, too;
These critters can get angry,
They'll take it out on you.

Be careful where you step,
You might get knocked down,
And if by chance you do,
Remember, don't roll around.

Those are dehornin' clippers
To snip off the horn bud,
Get 'em when they're little,
Careful, there's a bit of blood.

Take these shears and put
A notch in the left ear;
We brand and notch 'em, too,
So the owner's really clear.

Yeah, this ain't no picnic,
Watch out for the wire,
And yep, it smells like cattle
And the sun is hot as fire.

We turn bull calves into steers,
Shorty'll show you how it's done,
Don't be so squeamish now –
Here, he'll let you do one.

They're called mountain oysters,
You'll be mighty satisfied,
They're down right larrupin',
Rolled in batter and deep fried.

Toss 'em there in the bucket,
After we get through here,
We'll have a tasty cowboy feast,
Maybe a little whiskey and beer.

You look green-around-the-gills,
You need to cowboy up, for shore,
'Cause it's just a natural fact,
You ain't in New York anymore.

You Ain't
No Casey Tibbs

At our hometown rodeo,
Here's what they said to me:
"You ain't no Casey Tibbs,
You ain't never gonna be."

At the local pistol range,
Shootin' my old forty-five:
"You ain't no John Wayne,
No matter how you strive."

My critics were razor sharp:
"We've heard you try to sing,
And you ain't no Roy or Gene,
So don't do such a thing."

My feelin's were bruised and hurt,
I tried my level best to argue –
But all I could say was:
"Well, neither are any of you!"

You and I

Memories from the years,
I know them quite well,
Come to me again and again
Like the ringing of a bell.

If only we could return
And live it all once more,
You and I together
Thru life's open door.

When all memory fades
And thoughts from the past die,
I hope the last that I have
Are those of you and I

You Don't
Wanna Know

Billy Bob and Shorty,
Way out on the Texas plain,
Ridin' herd for the Bar X,
Scorchin' hot, needin' rain.

Billy Bob says to Shorty:
"Man on TV says every year
Gets hotter and hotter,
Arctic's startin' to disappear.

"This country'll be too hot
For man, beast or cow.
What'll it be like
Fifty or 100 years from how?"

"You don't wanna know,"
Was the reply.

"I made a trip into the city,"
Billy Bob says in despair,
"Cars and trucks and people
Rushin' about everywhere.

"Crowds and pollution,
Noise and blight all around;
In 50 or 100 years, what'll
It be like in town?"

"You don't wanna know,"
Was the reply.

"And cowhands like us
Are slowly fadin' away;
What'll it be like
Fifty or 100 years from today?"

"You don't wanna know,"
Was the reply.

"And in 50 or 100 years,
Will we keep from blowin'
The world into tiny bits,
The way things are goin'?"

"You **really** don't wanna know,"
Was the reply.

CPSIA information can be obtained
at www.ICGtesting.com
Printed in the USA
BVHW040502131119
563652BV00009BA/99/P